TWELVE MEDIEVAL THRESHOLDS

TWELVE MEDIEVAL THRESHOLDS

*A Structural History of the Medieval World
in Twelve Poems*

by J. A. Gucci
Instructor Edition

Pressure System Press
New York, New York

2026

Twelve Medieval Thresholds: A Structural History of the Medieval World in Twelve Poems
© 2026 J. A. Gucci

This book was composed according to the principles of Absolute Composition, a method of structural poetry based on one-to-one correspondence between natural systems and conceptual triads.

Epigraphs are drawn from historical sources in the public domain. Translations have been adapted where necessary for clarity and brevity.

Printed in the United States of America

First Edition

ISBN: 978-1-972788-16-5

www.jagucci.com

CONTENTS

Twelve Medieval Thresholds

A Structural History of the Medieval World in Twelve Poems

How to Use This Book

This book presents history through short poems organized around systems. Each poem models how a system forms, operates, or changes over time.

The poems are not meant to be interpreted in the traditional literary sense. Instead, they function as representations of structure. Each poem corresponds to a triad of related elements (for example: Land · Service · Protection) that together describe how a system operates.

The goal is not to ask what a poem "means," but to examine what the system does.

Each poem is paired with notes that provide:
• historical context
• a correspondence between the poem and a historical system
• discussion prompts aligned to the triad

Some steps within each system may not be stated directly. The system is complete, but not fully explained. Readers are expected to reconstruct how the process unfolds.

The poems may be used in a variety of settings:
• as brief openings to introduce a topic
• as points of comparison alongside historical material
• as prompts for discussion of cause and effect

- as models for describing systems in other domains

Because the poems are concise and highly compressed, they can be incorporated into a lesson, seminar, or independent study without replacing existing material. They are intended to clarify structure rather than add interpretive complexity.

At its core, this book presents history as a set of systems. By focusing on structure rather than interpretation, readers can more clearly understand how societies develop and change over time.

"No man is sufficient unto himself."

Instructor Notes

Poem Title: Virga
Triad: Land · Service · Protection

System Correspondence:

Medieval systems of landholding were structured around
conditional relationships. Land was not simply possessed; it
was granted in exchange for service, and protection depended
on the fulfillment of that obligation. These relationships were
often indirect and contingent, with outcomes shaped by
underlying conditions rather than surface appearances.

In the poem, rain falls on the forest floor—"rain on duff"—
suggesting wetness and stability. However, the presence of
"dry" indicates that the underlying layer remains flammable.
This corresponds to land: the base condition that appears
stable but contains hidden constraints.

The introduction of lightning corresponds to service: a
triggering interaction that activates the system. The response is
not immediate stability but transformation. The resulting
condition—"runoff"—reflects protection: a restructured system
in which the ground no longer absorbs water, but redirects it
across the surface.

Discussion Prompts:

Land: What conditions can exist beneath the surface of a
system that are not immediately visible?

Service: How do interactions or obligations activate change
within a system?

Protection: What results when a system no longer absorbs
pressure but redirects it?

Virga

Rain on duff—
dry

lightning
strike—

turpentine air—
runoff.

Instructor Notes

Poem Title: Field
Triad: Boundary · Labor · Yield

System Correspondence:

Medieval agricultural systems were defined by the relationship between land boundaries, labor, and production. Fields were not simply open spaces but structured areas where conditions, effort, and output were closely linked. The ability to produce depended on how boundaries were maintained and how labor acted within them.

In the poem, the opening condition—"pungent— / blue sheathing"—corresponds to boundary: an atmospheric layer that defines the conditions in which the system operates. The presence of ozone indicates an active boundary that interacts with incoming energy.

The introduction of the sun—"sun— / vapor"—corresponds to labor: energy acting upon the system to produce change. Solar input drives evaporation, transforming liquid water into vapor and initiating movement within the system.

The final condition—"rain"—corresponds to yield: the result of this interaction. Moisture returns to the ground, completing the cycle and producing conditions necessary for growth.

Discussion Prompts:

Boundary: How do environmental or structural limits shape what can occur within a system?

Labor: What role does energy or effort play in transforming conditions within a system?

Yield: What results from the interaction between conditions and labor?

Field

Pungent—
blue sheathing.

Sun—
vapor—

rain.

Instructor Notes

Poem Title: Granary
Triad: Surplus · Storage · Preservation

System Correspondence:

Medieval agricultural systems depended on the ability to retain resources beyond immediate use. Surplus production allowed communities to store food for periods of scarcity, but this required processes that prevented loss and maintained stability over time. Storage was not passive; it involved active measures to preserve accumulated resources.

In the poem, the opening condition—"green buds— / swelling peach"—corresponds to surplus: the accumulation of energy through growth. Sugars are produced and concentrated within the system, exceeding immediate need.

The transition—"red orange leaves / severed and sealed"— corresponds to storage: the system reduces loss by cutting off outward flow. Leaves are shed and vascular pathways are sealed, preventing the continued expenditure of energy.

The final condition—"furrows"—corresponds to preservation: the internal structure of the tree retains and contains stored resources. Energy is held within the organism through the winter, protected from depletion and prepared for future use.

Discussion Prompts:

Surplus: What conditions allow a system to produce more than it immediately uses?

Storage: How does a system prevent the loss of accumulated resources?

Preservation: What structures or processes allow resources to be retained over time?

Granary

Green buds—
swelling peach.

Red orange leaves—
severed and sealed—

furrows.

Instructor Notes

Poem Title: Oath
Triad: Lord · Vassal · Obligation

System Correspondence:

Medieval systems of authority were structured through reciprocal relationships. Lords granted access to resources, while vassals provided service and protection in return. These relationships were not linear exchanges but ongoing systems maintained through repeated interaction.

In the poem, the opening condition—"swollen thorn, / sugar stalk"—corresponds to lord: a source of resource within the system. The plant produces sugar, attracting other agents and establishing the basis for interaction.

The emergence of "swarm" corresponds to vassal: a group that gathers in response to available resources. Their presence is conditional, dependent on continued access to what is provided.

The action—"sting"—corresponds to obligation: the service performed in return. The ants defend the plant from external threats, reinforcing the stability of the system.

The return to "swollen thorn…" indicates that the system does not conclude but continues. Resource, response, and obligation form a loop, where each element sustains the others over time.

Discussion Prompts:

Lord: What role does a resource-providing entity play in structuring a system?

Vassal: How do dependent agents respond to access within a system?

Obligation: What actions sustain reciprocal relationships over time?

Oath

Swollen thorn,
sugar stalk.

Swarm—
sting—

swollen thorn…

Instructor Notes

Poem Title: Tithe
Triad: Production · Extraction · Redistribution

System Correspondence:

Medieval economic systems depended on the movement of
resources from sites of production to centralized institutions
and back into broader circulation. Tithes functioned as a
structured form of extraction, where a portion of what was
produced was collected and redistributed to support religious
and social systems.

In the poem, the opening condition—"zenith— / warm wet /
cool dry / air"—corresponds to production: the formation of
differentiated conditions within the system. Variations in
temperature and moisture create instability, allowing
movement to begin.

The motion—"rising— / sinking"—corresponds to extraction:
material is lifted and transported away from its point of origin.
Warm air rises, carrying moisture upward, while cooler air
descends, creating circulation within the system.

This circulation corresponds to redistribution: material is not
removed permanently but returned in altered form. The
system continuously transfers and reallocates resources
through movement, maintaining balance through repeated
exchange.

Discussion Prompts:

Production: What conditions allow resources to form or
accumulate within a system?

Extraction: How are resources removed or redirected from
their point of origin?

Redistribution: What results when resources are circulated and
returned within a system?

Tithe

Zenith—
warm and wet

rising cool
dry air—

sinking.

Instructor Notes

Poem Title: Fallow
Triad: Exhaustion · Rest · Renewal

System Correspondence:

Medieval agricultural systems required periods of non-use in order to remain productive. Continuous extraction of resources from the same land led to depletion, making rest necessary for long-term stability. Fallow periods allowed systems to recover, restoring the conditions needed for future production.

In the poem, the opening condition—"shrunk liver, / battered plumage"—corresponds to exhaustion: a system that has been depleted through sustained activity. Resources are diminished, and normal function is reduced.

The stillness—"still huddle"—corresponds to rest: a temporary suspension of activity that prevents further loss. The system withdraws from active use, conserving remaining energy.

The subsequent actions—"plunge dive— / preen oil"— correspond to renewal: processes that restore function and prepare the system for future activity. Energy is reorganized and redistributed, allowing recovery to occur.

Discussion Prompts:

Exhaustion: What happens when a system is used continuously without interruption?

Rest: How does the suspension of activity prevent further depletion?

Renewal: What processes allow a system to recover and regain function?

Fallow

Shrunk liver,
battered plumage.

Still huddle—
plunge dive—

preen oil.

Instructor Notes

Poem Title: Siege
Triad: Enclosure · Deprivation · Breach

System Correspondence:

Medieval warfare often involved sieges, where a fortified space was surrounded and isolated in order to force collapse from within. Rather than direct confrontation, control was exerted by restricting movement and access to resources. The outcome depended on how long the enclosed system could sustain itself under pressure.

In the poem, the opening condition—"mud wall / cell— / still"—corresponds to enclosure: a bounded system that restricts movement and isolates what is contained within. The structure defines a controlled interior space.

The tension—"vocal drums"—corresponds to deprivation: internal pressure builds as resources diminish and normal function is disrupted. Activity continues within the enclosure, but under increasing strain.

The final condition—"shell"—corresponds to breach: the system can no longer maintain its integrity and breaks. The enclosing structure fails, and what was contained is exposed or released.

Discussion Prompts:

Enclosure: How does restricting movement or access shape the behavior of a system?

Deprivation: What happens when a system is cut off from necessary resources?

Breach: What results when pressure exceeds the limits of a system's structure?

Siege

Mud wall
cell—

still—
vocal drums—

empty shell.

Instructor Notes

Poem Title: Pestilence
Triad: Density · Transmission · Collapse

System Correspondence:

Medieval outbreaks of disease spread through systems of proximity and contact. As populations became more concentrated, transmission increased, and the system could rapidly shift from stability to collapse. The spread of disease depended not only on the presence of a pathogen, but on the density and connectivity of the system.

In the poem, the opening condition—"crushed core— / neon" —corresponds to density: material is compressed into a concentrated state. This establishes the conditions necessary for rapid interaction and propagation.

The interaction—"buffet— / starlight"—corresponds to transmission: energy and material move outward from the core, spreading through the surrounding system. Contact and proximity allow the process to extend beyond its origin.

The final condition—"iron core— / supernova"—corresponds to collapse: the system reaches a threshold where internal pressure can no longer be contained, resulting in rapid and total breakdown..

Discussion Prompts:

Density: How does concentration within a system affect the likelihood of interaction or spread?

Transmission: What conditions allow a process to move through a system?

Collapse: What happens when a system exceeds its capacity to contain internal pressure?

Pestilence

Crushed core—
neon.

Buffet—
starlight.

Iron core—
supernova.

Instructor Notes

Poem Title: Abandonment
Triad: Use · Withdrawal · Reclaim

System Correspondence:

Medieval systems of settlement and land use were not always permanent. When resources were depleted or conditions changed, areas could be abandoned. Over time, these spaces were reshaped by natural processes, and new systems emerged in place of the old.

In the poem, the opening condition—"longshore waves— / battered island / shoreline"—corresponds to use: an actively shaped system influenced by continuous interaction. The coastline is formed and maintained through ongoing forces.

The disruption—"storm surge— / flume—"—corresponds to withdrawal: a forceful removal that alters the existing structure. Material is displaced, and the previous configuration is no longer sustained.

The final condition—"marsh peat"—corresponds to reclaim: a new system forms from what remains. Sediment accumulates, vegetation establishes, and the landscape reorganizes into a different, stable state.

Discussion Prompts:

Use: How does continuous interaction shape a system over time?

Withdrawal: What happens when sustaining forces are removed or disrupted?

Reclaim: How do new systems form after the breakdown or abandonment of previous ones?

Abandonment

Longshore waves—
battered island
shoreline—

high dune,
wide beach.

Storm surge—
flume—

marsh peat.

Instructor Notes

Poem Title: Guild
Triad: Skill · Constraint · Production

System Correspondence:

Medieval guilds organized production through specialized skill operating within defined constraints. Membership regulated who could produce, how work was performed, and how goods entered the system. These constraints structured output, but could also create pressure that led to expansion or change.

In the poem, the opening condition—"sand and silt / suspended— / dropped—"—corresponds to skill: the movement and placement of material within the system. Sediment is carried and deposited through controlled processes, shaping the initial structure.

The formation of "high banks— / narrow channel"— corresponds to constraint: the system becomes confined, directing movement through limited pathways. Flow is restricted, and structure is maintained through these boundaries.

The disruption—"broken, / breached— / forest"— corresponds to production: the system generates new land through the failure of its own constraints. When the channel can no longer contain the flow, material spreads outward, forming fertile ground that supports new growth.

Discussion Prompts:

Skill: How does specialized activity shape the structure of a system?

Constraint: What role do limits or regulations play in directing how a system operates?

Production: What results when a system exceeds or reorganizes its constraints?

Guild

Dropped—
sand and silt

High banks—
broken,

a narrow channel,
breached—

forest.

Instructor Notes

Poem Title: Road
Triad: Isolation · Connection · Exchange

System Correspondence:

Medieval systems of trade and communication depended on the ability to connect otherwise isolated regions. Roads allowed goods, information, and people to move between separate areas, transforming local systems into larger networks of exchange.

In the poem, the opening condition—"plunging plates— / trapped seawater—"—corresponds to isolation: distinct systems are separated and forced beneath one another. Movement is restricted, and material becomes confined within isolated regions.

The transformation—"liquid rock / channels"—corresponds to connection: material is reconfigured and begins to move through newly formed pathways. These channels allow interaction between previously separate areas.

The final condition—"erupting island / arc— / plankton"— corresponds to exchange: material rises and is redistributed across the surface, supporting new forms of activity. The system becomes interconnected, allowing transfer and interaction to occur.

Discussion Prompts:

Isolation: What conditions prevent interaction between parts of a system?

Connection: How are pathways formed that allow movement between separate areas?

Exchange: What results when systems become linked and material can move between them?

Road

Plunging plates—
swelling seawater—

liquid rock channels.
Erupting island arc—

plankton.

Instructor Notes

Poem Title: Compost
Triad: Waste · Breakdown · Fertility

System Correspondence:

Medieval systems depended on the reuse of materials that
were no longer immediately useful. Organic waste was not
discarded permanently but returned to the system, where it
was broken down and contributed to future production. This
process allowed resources to cycle rather than be lost.

In the poem, the opening condition—"marine snow"—
corresponds to waste: material that has fallen out of active use
and accumulates within the system. Organic matter settles and
becomes available for processing.

The transformation—"sea cucumber"—corresponds to
breakdown: material is consumed and processed by
detritivores. Through this process, complex matter is broken
down into forms that can be reintroduced into the system.

The final condition—"upwelling"—corresponds to fertility:
nutrients are returned to active circulation, supporting new
growth. The system is enriched by what has been broken
down, allowing continued productivity.

Discussion Prompts:

Waste: What materials fall out of active use within a system?

Breakdown: How are these materials consumed and
transformed within the system?

Fertility: What results when resources are returned to
circulation?

Compost

Marine snow—

sea cucumber —

upwelling.

Guide to Use

This book is designed to support the study of historical systems through concise, structured poems. Each poem can be used as a point of entry, comparison, or synthesis within a broader unit of study.

A typical use begins with close observation. The poem is read, and attention is directed toward condition, interaction, and change. From there, the corresponding system can be identified and connected to historical material.

The poems may be used in a variety of ways:
- to introduce a topic through a concrete system
- to accompany historical readings as a parallel model
- to support discussion of cause and effect
- to compare systems across different contexts
- to frame written or analytical responses

Because the poems are brief and highly compressed, they can be incorporated into a lesson, seminar, or independent study without replacing existing material. They function as tools for recognizing structure rather than as objects of interpretation.

Use may be adapted depending on context. The emphasis remains on identifying systems, reconstructing processes, and understanding how conditions produce outcomes.The Twelve Series

Each book in this series presents systems through short, structured poems.
Rather than describing events, the poems model how systems form, interact, and change over time.

Mesopotamia — formation
Egypt — stability
Greece — interaction
Rome — expansion and collapse

Each volume focuses on a different civilization, using the same method to reveal how complex societies develop.

Curriculum Placement

Typical Course Placement

This book aligns with courses that examine the medieval world, as well as broader studies of historical development, political organization, and economic systems.

It may be used within secondary or introductory postsecondary courses, as well as in interdisciplinary contexts that focus on systems, structure, or human-environment interaction.

Curriculum Connections

The poems correspond to major themes in medieval history:

- landholding and feudal relationships
- agricultural production and resource management
- systems of obligation and authority
- economic exchange and redistribution
- conflict, constraint, and structural pressure
- population dynamics and systemic collapse
- settlement, abandonment, and environmental change
- trade networks and connectivity
- material reuse and cyclical systems

Each poem models a system that reflects these developments, allowing readers to examine how conditions, interactions, and outcomes relate over time.

The material supports analysis of cause and effect, comparison across systems, and the study of how complex societies organize and transform.

Applied Exercise

This exercise uses the poems as fragments of a larger system.

Each poem may be approached as a partial record of a process. The task is to identify the system it represents and the transformation it describes.

Working individually or in groups, select a poem and determine:

• what transformation is occurring
• what system is being modeled
• what this reveals about the structure of the society

For example:

A poem such as Virga may be understood as:
condition → latent instability
interaction → ignition
result → system shift

A poem such as Granary may be understood as:
condition → accumulation
interaction → sealing
result → preservation

After analysis, multiple poems may be arranged in sequence. Viewed together, they form a progression of systems that reflect the development of a society.

The exercise may be adapted for discussion, written response, or comparative analysis. The emphasis remains on identifying structure, not interpreting symbolism.

Glossary

Virga — precipitation that does not fully wet the ground, leaving underlying conditions unchanged

Duff — a layer of decomposing organic material on the forest floor

Ozone — a reactive form of oxygen present in the atmosphere that interacts with solar radiation

Convection — movement within a fluid caused by temperature and density differences

Fallow — land left unworked to restore its productive capacity

Detritus — organic material that has fallen out of active use within a system

Sea cucumber — a marine organism that consumes and breaks down organic matter on the ocean floor

Upwelling — the movement of nutrient-rich water toward the surface

Sediment — particles transported and deposited by water or wind

Subduction — the movement of one tectonic plate beneath another

Succession — the process by which a system reorganizes and stabilizes over time

40

Appendix

The Triad Method

The poems in this book are organized around triads —groups of three related elements that describe how a system operates.

Rather than presenting history as a sequence of events, the triads focus on relationships between conditions, interactions, and outcomes. Each triad represents a process: a system that forms, changes, or stabilizes over time.

A triad may be understood as:
condition → what exists
interaction → what acts upon it
result → what emerges

In this book, some steps within each system are not fully stated. The systems are complete, but compressed. Readers are expected to reconstruct how the process unfolds.

The poems model these relationships using observable processes. The goal is not to interpret the poem, but to identify how the system functions.

This method can be applied beyond the book. Any system—historical, ecological, or social—can be examined by identifying three interacting elements that explain how it operates.

By focusing on structure rather than description,
the triads provide a way to understand how
complex systems develop and change.

The Twelve Series

Each book in this series presents systems through short, structured poems.

Rather than describing events, the poems model how systems form, operate, and change over time.

Each volume focuses on a different historical context while using the same underlying method. Together, they show how similar patterns appear across different environments and societies.

The books may be read individually or as a sequence. Viewed together, they reveal how systems develop, interact, and transform across time.

Twelve Clay Tablets: A Structural History of Mesopotamia in Twelve Poems

Twelve Desert Floods: A Structural History of Egypt in Twelve Poems

Twelve Marble Questions: A Structural History of Greece in Twelve Poems

Twelve Roman Thresholds: A Structural History of Rome in Twelve Poems

Twelve Medieval Thresholds: A Structural History of the Medieval World

Colophon

This book was set in a clear, readable typeface to
support close observation and sustained attention.

The poems follow a consistent structure to
emphasize condition, interaction, and change.

Designed and produced as part of the Twelve
series.

Composed according to the principles of Absolute
Composition, a method based on one-to-one
correspondence between natural systems and
conceptual triads.